PREPPING
PLANNER

Contents:

Emergency Information Sheet

Prepping Progress Sheet

Non-food Essentials Tick List

Water Inventory Pages

Meal Planner / Shopping List Pages- 52 weeks

Meal Inventory Pages- space for 365 days

(Breakfast / Lunch / Evening Meal)

Meal Planner Pages – space for 365 days

Recipe Ideas Pages

(to record your favourites)

Blank Inventory Pages

(use to keep track of other supplies e.g. pet food)

Blank Notes Pages

Prepping Tips

ISBN: 9781718128637

Emergency Information

Name: Telephone:

Address:

Emergency
contact: Telephone:

Useful Phone Numbers and Information

Family Member Contact Details	
Name	Telephone

Professional and Other Contact Details

Doctor:

Local Hospital:

Dentist:

Vet:

Police:

School:

House Insurance: Policy Number:

Car Insurance: Policy Number

Progress-Weeks Prepped For

Week 1 ☐ Week 2 ☐ Week 3 ☐ Week 4 ☐

Week 5 ☐ Week 6 ☐ Week 7 ☐ Week 8 ☐

Week 9 ☐ Week 10 ☐ Week 11 ☐ Week 12 ☐

Week 13 ☐ Week 14 ☐ Week 15 ☐ Week 16 ☐

Week 17 ☐ Week 18 ☐ Week 19 ☐ Week 20 ☐

Week 21 ☐ Week 22 ☐ Week 23 ☐ Week 24 ☐

Week 25 ☐ Week 26 ☐ Week 27 ☐ Week 28 ☐

Week 29 ☐ Week 30 ☐ Week 31 ☐ Week 32 ☐

Week 33 ☐ Week 34 ☐ Week 35 ☐ Week 36 ☐

Week 37 ☐ Week 38 ☐ Week 39 ☐ Week 40 ☐

Week 41 ☐ Week 42 ☐ Week 43 ☐ Week 44 ☐

Week 45 ☐ Week 46 ☐ Week 47 ☐ Week 48 ☐

Week 49 ☐ Week 50 ☐ Week 51 ☐ Week 52 ☐

Non-Food Essentials List

Water Inventory

Amount Added	Total	Amount Added	Total
–	O		

Water Inventory

Amount Added	Total	Amount Added	Total

Week 1:

	Breakfast	Lunch	Dinner	Notes
Mon				
Tues				
Weds				
Thurs				
Fri				
Sat				
Sun				

Water / Drinks / Snacks:

Shopping List

Recipe Info

Don't Forget

Week 2:

	Breakfast	Lunch	Dinner	Notes
Mon				
Tues				
Weds				
Thurs				
Fri				
Sat				
Sun				

Water / Drinks / Snacks:

Shopping List

Recipe Info

Don't Forget

Week 3:

	Breakfast	Lunch	Dinner	Notes
Mon				
Tues				
Weds				
Thurs				
Fri				
Sat				
Sun				

Water / Drinks / Snacks:

Shopping List

Recipe Info

Don't Forget

Week 4:

	Breakfast	Lunch	Dinner	Notes
Mon				
Tues				
Weds				
Thurs				
Fri				
Sat				
Sun				

Water / Drinks / Snacks:

Shopping List

Recipe Info

Don't Forget

Week 5:

	Breakfast	Lunch	Dinner	Notes
Mon				
Tues				
Weds				
Thurs				
Fri				
Sat				
Sun				

Water / Drinks / Snacks:

Shopping List

Recipe Info

Don't Forget

Week 6:

	Breakfast	Lunch	Dinner	Notes
Mon				
Tues				
Weds				
Thurs				
Fri				
Sat				
Sun				

Water / Drinks / Snacks:

Shopping List

Recipe Info

Don't Forget

Week 7:

	Breakfast	Lunch	Dinner	Notes
Mon				
Tues				
Weds				
Thurs				
Fri				
Sat				
Sun				

Water / Drinks / Snacks:

Shopping List

Recipe Info

Don't Forget

Week 8:

	Breakfast	Lunch	Dinner	Notes
Mon				
Tues				
Weds				
Thurs				
Fri				
Sat				
Sun				

Water / Drinks / Snacks:

Shopping List

Recipe Info

Don't Forget

Week 9:

	Breakfast	Lunch	Dinner	Notes
Mon				
Tues				
Weds				
Thurs				
Fri				
Sat				
Sun				

Water / Drinks / Snacks:

Shopping List

Recipe Info

Don't Forget

Week 10:

	Breakfast	Lunch	Dinner	Notes
Mon				
Tues				
Weds				
Thurs				
Fri				
Sat				
Sun				

Water / Drinks / Snacks:

Shopping List

Recipe Info

Don't Forget

Week 11:

	Breakfast	Lunch	Dinner	Notes
Mon				
Tues				
Weds				
Thurs				
Fri				
Sat				
Sun				

Water / Drinks / Snacks:

Shopping List

Recipe Info

Don't Forget

Week 12:

	Breakfast	Lunch	Dinner	Notes
Mon				
Tues				
Weds				
Thurs				
Fri				
Sat				
Sun				

Water / Drinks / Snacks:

Shopping List

Recipe Info

Don't Forget

Week 13:

	Breakfast	Lunch	Dinner	Notes
Mon				
Tues				
Weds				
Thurs				
Fri				
Sat				
Sun				

Water / Drinks / Snacks:

Shopping List

Recipe Info

Don't Forget

Week 14:

	Breakfast	Lunch	Dinner	Notes
Mon				
Tues				
Weds				
Thurs				
Fri				
Sat				
Sun				

Water / Drinks / Snacks:

Shopping List

Recipe Info

Don't Forget

Week 15:

	Breakfast	Lunch	Dinner	Notes
Mon				
Tues				
Weds				
Thurs				
Fri				
Sat				
Sun				

Water / Drinks / Snacks:

Shopping List

Recipe Info

Don't Forget

Week 16:

	Breakfast	Lunch	Dinner	Notes
Mon				
Tues				
Weds				
Thurs				
Fri				
Sat				
Sun				

Water / Drinks / Snacks:

Shopping List

Recipe Info

Don't Forget

Week 17:

	Breakfast	Lunch	Dinner	Notes
Mon				
Tues				
Weds				
Thurs				
Fri				
Sat				
Sun				

Water / Drinks / Snacks:

Shopping List

Recipe Info

Don't Forget

Week 18:

	Breakfast	Lunch	Dinner	Notes
Mon				
Tues				
Weds				
Thurs				
Fri				
Sat				
Sun				

Water / Drinks / Snacks:

Shopping List

Recipe Info

Don't Forget

Week 19:

	Breakfast	Lunch	Dinner	Notes
Mon				
Tues				
Weds				
Thurs				
Fri				
Sat				
Sun				

Water / Drinks / Snacks:

Shopping List

Recipe Info

Don't Forget

Week 20:

	Breakfast	Lunch	Dinner	Notes
Mon				
Tues				
Weds				
Thurs				
Fri				
Sat				
Sun				

Water / Drinks / Snacks:

Shopping List

Recipe Info

Don't Forget

Week 21:

	Breakfast	Lunch	Dinner	Notes
Mon				
Tues				
Weds				
Thurs				
Fri				
Sat				
Sun				

Water / Drinks / Snacks:

Shopping List

Recipe Info

Don't Forget

Week 22:

	Breakfast	Lunch	Dinner	Notes
Mon				
Tues				
Weds				
Thurs				
Fri				
Sat				
Sun				

Water / Drinks / Snacks:

Shopping List

Recipe Info

Don't Forget

Week 23:

	Breakfast	Lunch	Dinner	Notes
Mon				
Tues				
Weds				
Thurs				
Fri				
Sat				
Sun				

Water / Drinks / Snacks:

Shopping List

Recipe Info

Don't Forget

Week 24:

	Breakfast	Lunch	Dinner	Notes
Mon				
Tues				
Weds				
Thurs				
Fri				
Sat				
Sun				

Water / Drinks / Snacks:

Shopping List

Recipe Info

Don't Forget

Week 25:

	Breakfast	Lunch	Dinner	Notes
Mon				
Tues				
Weds				
Thurs				
Fri				
Sat				
Sun				

Water / Drinks / Snacks:

Shopping List

Recipe Info

Don't Forget

Week 26:

	Breakfast	Lunch	Dinner	Notes
Mon				
Tues				
Weds				
Thurs				
Fri				
Sat				
Sun				

Water / Drinks / Snacks:

Shopping List

Recipe Info

Don't Forget

Week 27:

	Breakfast	Lunch	Dinner	Notes
Mon				
Tues				
Weds				
Thurs				
Fri				
Sat				
Sun				

Water / Drinks / Snacks:

Shopping List

Recipe Info

Don't Forget

Week 28:

	Breakfast	Lunch	Dinner	Notes
Mon				
Tues				
Weds				
Thurs				
Fri				
Sat				
Sun				

Water / Drinks / Snacks:

Shopping List

Recipe Info

Don't Forget

Week 29:

	Breakfast	Lunch	Dinner	Notes
Mon				
Tues				
Weds				
Thurs				
Fri				
Sat				
Sun				

Water / Drinks / Snacks:

Shopping List

Recipe Info

Don't Forget

Week 30:

	Breakfast	Lunch	Dinner	Notes
Mon				
Tues				
Weds				
Thurs				
Fri				
Sat				
Sun				

Water / Drinks / Snacks:

Shopping List

Recipe Info

Don't Forget

Week 31:

	Breakfast	Lunch	Dinner	Notes
Mon				
Tues				
Weds				
Thurs				
Fri				
Sat				
Sun				

Water / Drinks / Snacks:

Shopping List

Recipe Info

Don't Forget

Week 32:

	Breakfast	Lunch	Dinner	Notes
Mon				
Tues				
Weds				
Thurs				
Fri				
Sat				
Sun				

Water / Drinks / Snacks:

Shopping List

Recipe Info

Don't Forget

Week 33:

	Breakfast	Lunch	Dinner	Notes
Mon				
Tues				
Weds				
Thurs				
Fri				
Sat				
Sun				

Water / Drinks / Snacks:

Shopping List

Recipe Info

Don't Forget

Week 34:

	Breakfast	Lunch	Dinner	Notes
Mon				
Tues				
Weds				
Thurs				
Fri				
Sat				
Sun				

Water / Drinks / Snacks:

Shopping List

Recipe Info

Don't Forget

Week 35:

	Breakfast	Lunch	Dinner	Notes
Mon				
Tues				
Weds				
Thurs				
Fri				
Sat				
Sun				

Water / Drinks / Snacks:

Shopping List

Recipe Info

Don't Forget

Week 36:

	Breakfast	Lunch	Dinner	Notes
Mon				
Tues				
Weds				
Thurs				
Fri				
Sat				
Sun				

Water / Drinks / Snacks:

Shopping List

Recipe Info

Don't Forget

Week 37:

	Breakfast	Lunch	Dinner	Notes
Mon				
Tues				
Weds				
Thurs				
Fri				
Sat				
Sun				

Water / Drinks / Snacks:

Shopping List

Recipe Info

Don't Forget

Week 38:

	Breakfast	Lunch	Dinner	Notes
Mon				
Tues				
Weds				
Thurs				
Fri				
Sat				
Sun				

Water / Drinks / Snacks:

Shopping List

Recipe Info

Don't Forget

Week 39:

	Breakfast	Lunch	Dinner	Notes
Mon				
Tues				
Weds				
Thurs				
Fri				
Sat				
Sun				

Water / Drinks / Snacks:

Shopping List

Recipe Info

Don't Forget

Week 40:

	Breakfast	Lunch	Dinner	Notes
Mon				
Tues				
Weds				
Thurs				
Fri				
Sat				
Sun				

Water / Drinks / Snacks:

Shopping List

Recipe Info

Don't Forget

Week 41:

	Breakfast	Lunch	Dinner	Notes
Mon				
Tues				
Weds				
Thurs				
Fri				
Sat				
Sun				

Water / Drinks / Snacks:

Shopping List

Recipe Info

Don't Forget

Week 42:

	Breakfast	Lunch	Dinner	Notes
Mon				
Tues				
Weds				
Thurs				
Fri				
Sat				
Sun				

Water / Drinks / Snacks:

Shopping List

Recipe Info

Don't Forget

Week 43:

	Breakfast	Lunch	Dinner	Notes
Mon				
Tues				
Weds				
Thurs				
Fri				
Sat				
Sun				

Water / Drinks / Snacks:

Shopping List

Recipe Info

Don't Forget

Week 44:

	Breakfast	Lunch	Dinner	Notes
Mon				
Tues				
Weds				
Thurs				
Fri				
Sat				
Sun				

Water / Drinks / Snacks:

Shopping List

Recipe Info

Don't Forget

Week 45:

	Breakfast	Lunch	Dinner	Notes
Mon				
Tues				
Weds				
Thurs				
Fri				
Sat				
Sun				

Water / Drinks / Snacks:

Shopping List

Recipe Info

Don't Forget

Week 46:

	Breakfast	Lunch	Dinner	Notes
Mon				
Tues				
Weds				
Thurs				
Fri				
Sat				
Sun				

Water / Drinks / Snacks:

Shopping List

Recipe Info

Don't Forget

Week 47:

	Breakfast	Lunch	Dinner	Notes
Mon				
Tues				
Weds				
Thurs				
Fri				
Sat				
Sun				

Water / Drinks / Snacks:

Shopping List

Recipe Info

Don't Forget

Week 48:

	Breakfast	Lunch	Dinner	Notes
Mon				
Tues				
Weds				
Thurs				
Fri				
Sat				
Sun				

Water / Drinks / Snacks:

Shopping List

Recipe Info

Don't Forget

Week 49:

	Breakfast	Lunch	Dinner	Notes
Mon				
Tues				
Weds				
Thurs				
Fri				
Sat				
Sun				

Water / Drinks / Snacks:

Shopping List

Recipe Info

Don't Forget

Week 50:

	Breakfast	Lunch	Dinner	Notes
Mon				
Tues				
Weds				
Thurs				
Fri				
Sat				
Sun				

Water / Drinks / Snacks:

Shopping List

Recipe Info

Don't Forget

Week 51:

	Breakfast	Lunch	Dinner	Notes
Mon				
Tues				
Weds				
Thurs				
Fri				
Sat				
Sun				

Water / Drinks / Snacks:

Shopping List

Recipe Info

Don't Forget

Week 52:

	Breakfast	Lunch	Dinner	Notes
Mon				
Tues				
Weds				
Thurs				
Fri				
Sat				
Sun				

Water / Drinks / Snacks:

Shopping List

Recipe Info

Don't Forget

Meal Inventory- Breakfast

#		#		#		#	
1		24		47		70	
2		25		48		71	
3		26		49		72	
4		27		50		73	
5		28		51		74	
6		29		52		75	
7		30		53		76	
8		31		54		77	
9		32		55		78	
10		33		56		79	
11		34		57		80	
12		35		58		81	
13		36		59		82	
14		37		60		83	
15		38		61		84	
16		39		62		85	
17		40		63		86	
18		41		64		87	
19		42		65		88	
20		43		66		89	
21		44		67		90	
22		45		68		91	
23		46		69		92	

Meal Inventory- Breakfast

93		116		139		162	
94		117		140		163	
95		118		141		164	
96		119		142		165	
97		120		143		166	
98		121		144		167	
99		122		145		168	
100		123		146		169	
101		124		147		170	
102		125		148		171	
103		126		149		172	
104		127		150		173	
105		128		151		174	
106		129		152		175	
107		130		153		176	
108		131		154		177	
109		132		155		178	
110		133		156		179	
111		134		157		180	
112		135		158		181	
113		136		159		182	
114		137		160		183	
115		138		161		184	

Meal Inventory- Breakfast

185		208		231		254	
186		209		232		255	
187		210		233		256	
188		211		234		257	
189		212		235		258	
190		213		236		259	
191		214		237		260	
192		215		238		261	
193		216		239		262	
194		217		240		263	
195		218		241		264	
196		219		242		265	
197		220		243		266	
198		221		244		267	
199		222		245		268	
200		223		246		269	
201		224		247		270	
202		225		248		271	
203		226		249		272	
204		227		250		273	
205		228		251		274	
206		229		252		275	
207		230		253		276	

Meal Inventory- Breakfast

277		300		323		346	
278		301		324		347	
279		302		325		348	
280		303		326		349	
281		304		327		350	
282		305		328		351	
283		306		329		352	
284		307		330		353	
285		308		331		354	
286		309		332		355	
287		310		333		356	
288		311		334		357	
289		312		335		358	
290		313		336		359	
291		314		337		360	
292		315		338		361	
293		316		339		362	
294		317		340		363	
295		318		341		364	
296		319		342		365	
297		320		343			
298		321		344			
299		322		345			

Meal Inventory- Lunch

#		#		#		#	
1		24		47		70	
2		25		48		71	
3		26		49		72	
4		27		50		73	
5		28		51		74	
6		29		52		75	
7		30		53		76	
8		31		54		77	
9		32		55		78	
10		33		56		79	
11		34		57		80	
12		35		58		81	
13		36		59		82	
14		37		60		83	
15		38		61		84	
16		39		62		85	
17		40		63		86	
18		41		64		87	
19		42		65		88	
20		43		66		89	
21		44		67		90	
22		45		68		91	
23		46		69		92	

Meal Inventory- Lunch

93		116		139		162	
94		117		140		163	
95		118		141		164	
96		119		142		165	
97		120		143		166	
98		121		144		167	
99		122		145		168	
100		123		146		169	
101		124		147		170	
102		125		148		171	
103		126		149		172	
104		127		150		173	
105		128		151		174	
106		129		152		175	
107		130		153		176	
108		131		154		177	
109		132		155		178	
110		133		156		179	
111		134		157		180	
112		135		158		181	
113		136		159		182	
114		137		160		183	
115		138		161		184	

Meal Inventory- Lunch

185		208		231		254	
186		209		232		255	
187		210		233		256	
188		211		234		257	
189		212		235		258	
190		213		236		259	
191		214		237		260	
192		215		238		261	
193		216		239		262	
194		217		240		263	
195		218		241		264	
196		219		242		265	
197		220		243		266	
198		221		244		267	
199		222		245		268	
200		223		246		269	
201		224		247		270	
202		225		248		271	
203		226		249		272	
204		227		250		273	
205		228		251		274	
206		229		252		275	
207		230		253		276	

Meal Inventory- Lunch

277		300		323		346	
278		301		324		347	
279		302		325		348	
280		303		326		349	
281		304		327		350	
282		305		328		351	
283		306		329		352	
284		307		330		353	
285		308		331		354	
286		309		332		355	
287		310		333		356	
288		311		334		357	
289		312		335		358	
290		313		336		359	
291		314		337		360	
292		315		338		361	
293		316		339		362	
294		317		340		363	
295		318		341		364	
296		319		342		365	
297		320		343			
298		321		344			
299		322		345			

Meal Inventory- Evening Meal

1		24		47		70	
2		25		48		71	
3		26		49		72	
4		27		50		73	
5		28		51		74	
6		29		52		75	
7		30		53		76	
8		31		54		77	
9		32		55		78	
10		33		56		79	
11		34		57		80	
12		35		58		81	
13		36		59		82	
14		37		60		83	
15		38		61		84	
16		39		62		85	
17		40		63		86	
18		41		64		87	
19		42		65		88	
20		43		66		89	
21		44		67		90	
22		45		68		91	
23		46		69		92	

Meal Inventory- Evening Meal

93		116		139		162	
94		117		140		163	
95		118		141		164	
96		119		142		165	
97		120		143		166	
98		121		144		167	
99		122		145		168	
100		123		146		169	
101		124		147		170	
102		125		148		171	
103		126		149		172	
104		127		150		173	
105		128		151		174	
106		129		152		175	
107		130		153		176	
108		131		154		177	
109		132		155		178	
110		133		156		179	
111		134		157		180	
112		135		158		181	
113		136		159		182	
114		137		160		183	
115		138		161		184	

Meal Inventory- Evening Meal

185		208		231		254	
186		209		232		255	
187		210		233		256	
188		211		234		257	
189		212		235		258	
190		213		236		259	
191		214		237		260	
192		215		238		261	
193		216		239		262	
194		217		240		263	
195		218		241		264	
196		219		242		265	
197		220		243		266	
198		221		244		267	
199		222		245		268	
200		223		246		269	
201		224		247		270	
202		225		248		271	
203		226		249		272	
204		227		250		273	
205		228		251		274	
206		229		252		275	
207		230		253		276	

Meal Inventory- Evening Meal

277		300		323		346	
278		301		324		347	
279		302		325		348	
280		303		326		349	
281		304		327		350	
282		305		328		351	
283		306		329		352	
284		307		330		353	
285		308		331		354	
286		309		332		355	
287		310		333		356	
288		311		334		357	
289		312		335		358	
290		313		336		359	
291		314		337		360	
292		315		338		361	
293		316		339		362	
294		317		340		363	
295		318		341		364	
296		319		342		365	
297		320		343			
298		321		344			
299		322		345			

Meal Planner

Day	Bfast	Lunch	Dinner	Day	Bfast	Lunch	Dinner
1				27			
2				28			
3				29			
4				30			
5				31			
6				32			
7				33			
8				34			
9				35			
10				36			
11				37			
12				38			
13				39			
14				40			
15				41			
16				42			
17				43			
18				44			
19				45			
20				46			
21				47			
22				48			
23				49			
24				50			
25				51			
26				52			

Meal Planner

Day	Bfast	Lunch	Dinner	Day	Bfast	Lunch	Dinner
53				79			
54				80			
55				81			
56				82			
57				83			
58				84			
59				85			
60				86			
61				87			
62				88			
63				89			
64				90			
65				91			
66				92			
67				93			
68				94			
69				95			
70				96			
71				97			
72				98			
73				99			
74				100			
75				101			
76				102			
77				103			
78				104			

Meal Planner

Day	Bfast	Lunch	Dinner
105			
106			
107			
108			
109			
110			
111			
112			
113			
114			
115			
116			
117			
118			
119			
120			
121			
122			
123			
124			
125			
126			
127			
128			
129			
130			

Day	Bfast	Lunch	Dinner
131			
132			
133			
134			
135			
136			
137			
138			
139			
140			
141			
142			
143			
144			
145			
146			
147			
148			
149			
150			
151			
152			
153			
154			
155			
156			

Meal Planner

Day	Bfast	Lunch	Dinner	Day	Bfast	Lunch	Dinner
157				183			
158				184			
159				185			
160				186			
161				187			
162				188			
163				189			
164				190			
165				191			
166				192			
167				193			
168				194			
169				195			
170				196			
171				197			
172				198			
173				199			
174				200			
175				201			
176				202			
177				203			
178				204			
179				205			
180				206			
181				207			
182				208			

Meal Planner

Day	Bfast	Lunch	Dinner
209			
210			
211			
212			
213			
214			
215			
216			
217			
218			
219			
220			
221			
222			
223			
224			
225			
226			
227			
228			
229			
230			
231			
232			
233			
234			

Day	Bfast	Lunch	Dinner
235			
236			
237			
238			
239			
240			
241			
242			
243			
244			
245			
246			
247			
248			
249			
250			
251			
252			
253			
254			
255			
256			
257			
258			
259			
260			

Meal Planner

Day	Bfast	Lunch	Dinner	Day	Bfast	Lunch	Dinner
261				287			
262				288			
263				289			
264				290			
265				291			
266				292			
267				293			
268				294			
269				295			
270				296			
271				297			
272				298			
273				299			
274				300			
275				301			
276				302			
277				303			
278				304			
279				305			
280				306			
281				307			
282				308			
283				309			
284				310			
285				311			
286				312			

Meal Planner

Day	Bfast	Lunch	Dinner
313			
314			
315			
316			
317			
318			
319			
320			
321			
322			
323			
324			
325			
326			
327			
328			
329			
330			
331			
332			
333			
334			
335			
336			
337			
338			

Day	Bfast	Lunch	Dinner
339			
340			
341			
342			
343			
344			
345			
346			
347			
348			
349			
350			
351			
352			
353			
354			
355			
356			
357			
358			
359			
360			
361			
362			
363			
364			
365			

Recipe Ideas

Inventory-

Amount Added	Total	Amount Added	Total
–	0		

Inventory-

Amount Added	Total	Amount Added	Total
–	0		

Inventory-

Amount Added	Total	Amount Added	Total
–	O		

Inventory-

Amount Added	Total	Amount Added	Total
–	0		

Notes

Prepping Tips

Think of meal ideas that can be made using ingredients with long shelf life.

Make sure you only buy food to make meals that you like and will eat.

Cycle your stored food through your normal eating to ensure it doesn't go out of date.

Meal Plan- this will help you buy food more cheaply as you will not have leftovers and to allow you to plan a varied diet.

Don't rely on one storage method- freezers are great but if the power goes off so do they. Have meals planned that use ingredients from different storage methods in case your freezer goes down.

Buy at least one spare tin opener.

Make sure you have some meals stored that can be eaten hot or cold in case the power goes off and you can't cook.

Consider alternative cooking methods- is getting a camping stove a safe option in case of emergency?

Think about how you store your food- you don't want it in sight of visitors.

Don't tell people you are storing food- if people get hungry in the event of food shortages it could make you a target.

Consider trading down brands to make your food stockpiling more affordable.

Try to store a few treats- if food shortages of and you have to use your store, some treats will be good for morale.

Don't forget to buy plenty of water.

Made in the USA
Columbia, SC
04 May 2019